POEMS

ON

Several Subjects:

Written by

STEPHEN DUCK,

Lately a poor *Thresher* in a Barn in the County of *Wilts*, at the Wages of Four Shillings and Sixpence *per* Week:

Which were publickly read by

The Right Honourable the Earl of *Macclesfield,* in the Drawing-Room at *Windsor*-Castle, on *Friday* the 11th of *September*, 1730, to her MAJESTY.

Who was thereupon moſt graciouſly pleaſed to take the Author into her Royal Protection, by allowing him a Salary of Thirty Pounds *per Annum*, and a ſmall Houſe at *Richmond* in *Surrey*, to live in, for the better Support of Himſelf and Family.

The SEVENTH EDITION, Corrected.

To which is added,

Some Account of the LIFE of the AUTHOR.

LONDON:

Printed for J. ROBERTS, near the *Oxford-Arms* in *Warwick-Lane*; and Sold by the Bookſellers of *London* and *Weſtminſter*. M.DCC.XXX.

Price Six Pence.

THE THRESHER'S LABOUR
THE WOMAN'S LABOUR

Stephen Duck.

The Thresher's Labour
by Stephen Duck

The Woman's Labour
by Mary Collier

Two Eighteenth Century Poems

Introduction by E.P. Thompson

Illustrations by Marian Sugden

Edited by E.P. Thompson & Marian Sugden

THE MERLIN PRESS
LONDON

Set by Hems & Co, Gillingham, Dorset
and printed by Whitstable Litho Printers Ltd
Whitstable, Kent

INTRODUCTION

These poems should be more widely known and enjoyed than they are. Stephen Duck's is still remembered, but Mary Collier's is known only to a few specialists. Both are vigorous poems in which a way of livelihood is imaginatively realised. Both betray cultural insecurities when they attempt to follow the polite models of the time, and then recover authenticity when the details of habitual labour take us into places for which the polite culture provides little precedent.

Both poems are about daily labour. It is interesting that, in each case, this is the best poem that the poet wrote. Duck wrote and published a good deal, but the rest of his output is deservedly forgotten, and much the same is true of the small published output of Collier. This is not just a judgement from the standpoint of social history—although, obviously, authentic accounts of labour by labourers have a particular interest. It is also the case that the poets' feelings were far more directly engaged when they reflected on threshing or on laundering than when they turned to approved 'poetic' themes, and in the case of 'The Woman's Labour', the gender polemic gives an additional lift and wit to the lines.

Stephen Duck was born in 1705 in Great Charlton in Wiltshire. His family was, perhaps, of 'husbandman' or upper labouring status, aspiring to be yeomen. Stephen was sent to a local charity school. By one account he was learning so fast that his 'prudent Parent . . . removed her Son from School to the Plow, lest he might become too fine a Gentleman for the Family that produced him.' By another (and more reliable) account he attended until he was 14—a late school-age for a labourer's child. He worked for a while with his father, who for a short time was able to rent a small farm. Then he went into service, living-in with one farmer or another. When he married in 1724 he presumably took a cottage of his own, where two sons and a daughter were born to his wife Ann. Early editions of his poems describe him as 'lately a poor thresher', with a weekly wage of 4s 6d.

At about the time of his marriage he set about his self-education, in such time as he could snatch from work, sometimes setting to his books late at night, sometimes sitting down 'all over Sweat and Heat' to read in an interval of labour. From arithmetic he graduated to poetry. He had a friend who had been in service in London, and who had a library of two or three dozen books, which included some volumes of the *Spectator*, a translation of 'Seneca's Morals', and *Paradise Lost*. He also bought and borrowed other books, including an odd volume of Shakespeare (with seven plays), Dryden's 'Virgil', Bysshe's *Art of Poetry*, Butler's 'Hudibras', and some Addison. There was also some Ovid in translation and the *London Spy*.

We owe knowledge of this reading to the Reverend Joseph Spence, Professor of Poetry at Oxford University, who spent the better part of a week talking with Duck in 1730. Duck had delighted in ballads and in singing from his childhood, but the acquisition of polite literature required an essay in translation. He pored over the works with Bailey's dictionary and an English grammar beside him, and, in Spence's words,

> He has got English just as we get Latin. Most of his Language in Conversation, as well as in his Poems, is acquir'd by reading . . . His common Talk is made up of the good Stile, with a mixture of the Rustick.

He was soon writing verses, and burning them, and by 1729 (when he was twenty-four) he was being talked about as a local wonder. When his third child was christened one of the women attending boasted to the officiating clergyman that 'Mr Duck was a Man of great Learning, and had Wit enough to be a Parson.' Several clergy and local gentry became interested, suggested themes to him, and his verses 'were handed about the Country with great Applause in Manuscript'. He was even 'admitted to the Tables of a great many worthy Gentlemen'. His reputation rested less upon 'The Thresher's Labour' than upon 'The Shunammite'; a formal literary production based on the Book of Kings, 2, IV which earned high praise from Joseph Spence for its epic machinery and observance of proprieties.

The genius in the threshing barn became a theme of genteel conversation and a target for competitive patronage. When the Earl of Macclesfield visited Hampshire

in the summer of 1730 he 'sent for' Duck. Dr Alured
Clarke, Prebendary of Winchester Cathedral, took a
particular and possessive interest in the thresher poet. He
had highly-placed friends, including Mrs Clayton (subse-
quently Lady Sundon), an influential lady-in-waiting to
Queen Caroline. Dr Clarke sent Duck's poems to
Mrs Clayton, who told the queen about the rustic genius
and (on September 11th) the Earl of Macclesfield read
some of the verses to Caroline. 'Her Majesty resolv'd
immediately to take him out of his obscurity,' and he was
summoned to her presence.

Dr Clarke's letters to Mrs Clayton survive, and they
show how the two of them were managing this interesting
affair. The queen had already indicated that she would
settle an income on Stephen Duck, who would at first be
employed in some gardening at Kew and in repairing his
deficient education. On September 19, Dr Clarke wrote
from Winchester that he had had 'the Thresher' with him
all week, preparing him for Her Majesty's bounty. He
would send Duck to Windsor in a fortnight, but his family
would follow afterwards 'when he is settled and ready to
receive them'. An additional sum had been gathered for
him, but Duck had 'promised not to meddle with any of
the money'. Clarke advised that the money (which he
was sending on to Mrs Clayton) 'should be put out upon
security for the benefit of his family, or for his own use, if
misconduct or any other accident should make it expedient
for him to return into Wiltshire'. It seems that the elevation
of 'poor Stephen' (as these correspondents sometimes
referred to him) was probationary and conditional upon
his good conduct. Clarke further advised that Duck should
read in the theory of horticulture, for 'then he will be sure
of a provision for his family if his muse should forsake him'.

On October 4th Stephen Duck was at length despatched—
not (as it seemed best on second thoughts) to the Court at
Windsor but to Kew. He seems to have been concerned
about his wife (of whom 'he speaks so well') and he
planned to return soon and fetch his family with him. He
was accompanied and followed by letters to Mrs Clayton
in which Clarke advised as to his reading. He must be
given Burnet's *Theory of the Earth*, Ray's *Wisdom of God
in the Creation*, and Dr Clark's *Rohault*, which would

introduce him to 'Descartes' System'. He must also get Pope's *Essay on Criticism* by heart, and Clarke even sent on a note of introduction to Pope—not because he approved of such a disloyal fellow but because 'it would be prudent not to expose [Duck] to the malice of the Dunciad Club'. Clarke's next letter gave further advice on reading, and his next (October 15) enclosed an account, from a farmer in Duck's village, of the death of Stephen's wife, Ann. In response the Prebendary lied to the farmer, saying he was not certain where Stephen Duck was; and, in a letter to Duck, he made no mention of the small matter that his wife had died, since (he explained to Mrs Clayton) 'I could not be sure you would think it proper to deject him with such ill news before Her Majesty had seen him . . .' Clarke had placed Duck completely in Mrs Clayton's charge, and no doubt he would be returned to his bereaved family 'whenever you think proper to send him'. Clarke supposed that Duck would board his children out somewhere in the country. (At least one of his two sons was to be schooled at Eton). Ten days later (October 25th) Dr Clarke's spirits had risen once more. Ann's death might stimulate Stephen to produce verses worthy of the queen's patronage; 'I do not know but what we may promise ourselves one of his best strains of poetry on this occasion, from the natural and constant correspondence there is between the mind and the affections'. Patronage of this order is simply a form taken by the conspiracy of the polite against the poor.

Queen Caroline granted to Duck £30 (and perhaps more) per annum and a small house in Richmond, close to her own favourite residence at Richmond Lodge. A tutor was found to help 'poor Stephen' in the Latin tongue. But Dr Clarke advised—despite the pirated editions of Duck's poems—that there should be a delay in any authorised edition, since this 'may give him time to make considerable alterations in what he has done . . .' Duck had been extracted in one moment from his home, his occupation, his community, and also his family; and his patrons were doing their best to tame and make polite his muse.

Some social drama was going on which it is difficult now to interpret. In one sense Stephen Duck's story dramatises the almost unbridgeable gap which had developed in the early eighteenth century between polite and plebeian cultures. The early editions of Duck's poems (1730, 1731 and 1733) were all pirated, and they include an unauthorised biographical note in which someone who pretended to Duck's acquaintance described how his wife, Ann, was always scolding him for neglecting his labour, 'and when he was Scanning his Lines, she would often-times run out and raise the whole Neighbourhood, telling them "that her Husband dealt with the Devil, and was going mad because he did nothing all day but talk to himself, and tell his Fingers".' True or false (it was probably false) the story is symptomatic of the times; it stereotypes what the gulf between the 'good Stile' and 'the Rustick' was supposed to be. On the other hand, this gulf was not quite unbridgeable. Genius could take wing and fly across. A sardonic critic (possibly Pope) noted of Stephen Duck's first appearances at Queen Caroline's court—

> All the Wits and Criticks of the Court flock'd about him, delighted to see a *Clown* with a ruddy hale Complexion and in his own long Hair, so top-full of Poetry; and at the first sight of him all agreed he was born to be *Poet Laureate*.

Contradictory impulses were at work. The genteel were wary of enthusiasm and the strategies of the polite culture were intended to discourage the uncultivated and the rude. In the 1730s there was little Romantic yearning for the primitive. Yet at a time when nearly every genteel accomplishment went about in wigs, there was at least novelty in encountering a poet in his own hair and speaking in an unclassical tongue. And since Duck had made painstaking efforts to cultivate himself, he was an estimable object of patronage. Joseph Spence wrote to Pope that "Tis a Man without anything of what is cald Education, grown up into an Excellent Poet all at once . . . One sees the Strugles of a great Soul in him . . . his Ignorance as he manages it has something even agreeable in it.' (Pope thought little of Duck's verse, but he told Gay that the man was 'harmless', and they seem to have co-existed at Richmond agreeably as neighbours).

The discovery and patronage of merit reflected honour also on the patron. Queen Caroline was no judge of English poetry; she was German by birth, she conversed with her family in French, and her command of English was always imperfect. But she was a good judge of the gestures of patronage, at a time when ostentatious liberality was part of the necessary public image of the great.

The list of subscribers at the front of the 1736 edition of Duck's *Poems on Several Occasions* is headed by His Royal Highness the Prince of Wales, and includes four princesses, seventeen dukes and duchesses, forty-three countesses, earls, marquises and viscounts, the archbishops of Canterbury and of York and eight other bishops, three Lord Chief Justices, the Master of the Rolls, Sir Robert Walpole, the Speaker of the House of Commons, the Recorder of the City of London, thirty-nine Ladies, thirty-seven Lords, a multitude of baronets, gentry and clergy, and even a few humble mortals who included Alexander Pope and Jonathan Swift. It is a remarkable subscription, and it suggests that the modest and mild-mannered Duck had made few personal enemies. It also suggests that the subscribers thought it politic to stand well with Duck's patron, Queen Caroline. Lord Palmerston extended the gesture of patronage from the individual to the class, by appropriating the rent of an acre of land to provide an annual dinner and strong beer to the threshers of Charlton in honour of their former comrade—a dinner which Duck himself once attended.

What Stephen Duck thought about all this it is not possible to know. He did say that gentlemen might like his poems 'because they were made by a poor Fellow in a Barn'. But before his sudden translation to the court, the poet he most 'admired and doted on' was Milton, a poet who did not write in a wig. (It is said that Duck had committed most of *Paradise Lost* to memory.) From the time of his elevation, notions of propriety elbowed aside the Miltonic impulse. Duck was prompted, advised on his reading, educated in the classics, and made a yeoman of the guard. He married Sarah Big, Queen Caroline's housekeeper at Kew Green. The queen constructed an ornate grotto called 'Merlin's Cave', supplied with a collection of books, and Duck was appointed librarian and caretaker. He became an object of envy to the unpatronised, and of more general ridicule. Swift wrote:

> The thresher, Duck, could o'er the Queen prevail:
> The proverb says, no fence against a flail.
> From *threshing* corn, he turns to *thresh* his brains,
> For which her Majesty allows him *grains*:
> Tho' 'tis confest, that those who ever saw
> His poems, think them all not worth *a straw*.

From the moment that he left the thresher's barn it was downhill all the way. Of his subsequent verse Raymond Williams has written (in *The Country and the City*) that 'it is easy to feel the strain of this labourer's voice as it adapts, slowly, to the available models in verse: the formal explanation, the anxious classical reference, the arranged subordinate clauses of that self-possessed literary manner'. This is well said, but I cannot agree that the adaptation is slow. Duck capitulated at once to whatever his patrons expected or advised, presenting them with self-deprecating, mannered, and sometimes abjectly deferential poems. He also wrote occasional pieces ('To His Royal Highness, the Duke of Cumberland, on his [twelfth] Birth-Day') as the Queen's unofficial laureate. It is not (John Lucas has written) that Duck's poems are incompetent. He works hard at mastering the modes and proprieties of the time, and his poems read like accomplished exercises or studied imitations of approved forms—Pindarics, Horatian Odes, epistles and the rest; but 'poem after poem contains its unsurprisingly apt classical allusion, its stock simile, its tamely generalised diction'. In one of his better exercises ('To Death—An Irregular Ode') he confessed:

> I, like the rest, advance my Lays;
> With uncouth Numbers, rumble forth a Song,
> Sedately dull, to celebrate thy Praise;
> And lash, and spur the heavy lab'ring Muse along.

The best of his later poems may be 'A Description of a Journey to Marlborough, Bath, Portsmouth, &c', in which, amidst ingratiating passages to patrons, there is a humdrum authenticity of a travel journal, and, as when he tries his hand at mowing once more, a stirring of regret at his life's translation. In 1746 he was ordained in the Church of England; he drew large congregations as a preacher at Kew Chapel, and he became Rector of Byfleet in Surrey in 1752. In 1756 he drowned himself in some water behind

'The Black Lion' in Reading.

'The Thresher's Labour' commences firmly in a capitalist countryside. The substantial tenant farmer is counting 'the Profits of the Year', but is anxious about paying 'threat'ning Landlord's Rent'. The farmer 'calls his Threshers forth', and the labourers are clearly tied by bonds of obligation as well as need to the farmer. The labour appears to be at day or week rates, and discipline is maintained by the direct surveillance of the employer. Duck's description of threshing disabuses us of any notion that 'mechanical' and repetitive labour must await the coming of industrialism and the production-line.

The hay harvest commences light-heartedly and competitively, but soon it also assumes its own monotony. In the brief interval between the hay and cereal harvest, those labourers who are also threshers (and therefore have some permanence on the farm's labour force) return to their work in the barns. At cereal harvest, once again vigour and enthusiasm give way to exhaustion:

> Before us we perplexing Thistles find,
> And Corn blown adverse with the ruffling Wind:
> Behind our Backs the Female Gleaners wait,
> Who sometimes stoop, and sometimes hold a Chat . . .

We end with the obligatory set-piece of the carrying-in of the harvest, followed by the harvest-home supper with the ritual inversion of social orders as the master serves his own labourers. 'But the next morning soon reveals the Cheat.'

Duck's poem reveals that the women perform only light, marginal contributions in this epic of arduous male labour. The women may remain in their cottages, to be scared by the sooty appearance of the labourers when they return from threshing peas. Or, when the women come into the farmer's hayfield, they are 'prattling Females' who are—

> Prepar'd, whilst he is here, to make his Hay;
> Or, if he turns his Back, prepar'd to play . . .

They gossip like sparrows, waste time, and when they run for shelter in the rain-storm this provides light relief in Duck's sombre poem. Even when they are gleaning, they stop to chat. Men had long known about the deficiencies of female labour, and Duck's poem confirmed this knowledge. Who, after all, would know better than a Wiltshire thresher?

Well, perhaps a woman labourer might? Duck's poem annoyed Mary Collier, a Hampshire washer-woman, enough to inspire her to a reply, which was first published in 1739. Predictably, when 'The Woman's Labour' was first published there was speculation that the poem had been written by a man—perhaps even by Stephen Duck. But Mary Collier did exist. She was born in the late 17th century, so that when her poem was published she was over fifty. She started life near Midhurst, in Sussex; never went to school; but was taught to read when very young by her mother, upon whose early death she 'lost her education'. She continued to read as 'recreation', and the little account that we have of her reading suggests that its staple was the works of pious Protestantism—Fox's *Book of Martyrs* and his *Acts and Monuments*, Speed and Baker's *Chronicles* and Flavius Josephus's *Works*—variants on Old Testament history and the early records of the Jews. But she probably also had access to those other staples of the commoners' reading—almanacs, chapbooks and the like, for she confessed that when young 'any foolish History highly delighted me'.

Mary Collier spent the years of her first vigour in looking after her ailing father, alongside such occasional employment 'as the Country afforded'. She did not marry, and on her father's death she moved to Petersfield in Hampshire where she worked as a washer-woman and itinerant household brewer until the age of sixty-three. Then she went for a few more years to be housekeeper at a farm near Alton. She is last heard of, in her seventy-second year, writing a bad poem in honour of the marriage of George III. She had then retired to a 'garret' in Alton, where she was 'endeavouring to pass the Relict of my days in Piety, Purity, Peace, and an Old Maid'.

There was no dramatic life-translation for Mary Collier. A few local gentlewomen and gentry gave her a little support, and an edition of her poems, published in Winchester in 1762, was endorsed by a substantial list of subscribers. But 'The Woman's Labour' earned her no further preferment. As she had predicted—

> For all our Pains, no Prospect can we see
> Attend us, but Old Age and Poverty.

Collier's poem is a telling critique, in the old folk-mode of the 'argument of the sexes', of Duck's male prejudice:

> Those mighty Troubles which perplex your Mind,
> (*Thistles* before, and *Females* come behind) . . .

But her rejoinder to Duck is witty rather than hostile. Indeed, when 'The Thresher's Labour' first appeared she got the poem by heart, until 'fancying he had been too Severe on the Female Sex . . . brought me to a Strong propensity to call an Army of Amazons to vidicate the injured Sex'. She answered 'The Thresher's Labour' 'to please my own humour, little thinking to make it Public'. 'It lay by me several Years and by now and then repeating a few lines to amuse myself and entertain my Company, it got Air.' A gentlewoman whom she nursed through an illness, and her friends, encouraged Collier further until her verses 'became a Town Talk'. Perhaps (as with Duck) these patrons did a little to polish the poems for publication, but there is no evidence of serious interference.

Although Collier herself was single, her poem is a forceful statement of the married woman's dual roles. After a day's haymaking, she returns to prepare dinner for her labouring husband, to feeding the pigs and attending to the children. In cereal harvest, she reaps, gathers or gleans. The infants are carried to the fields and tended in between spells of labour. The second part of the poem describes Collier's own occupation of 'charing' (washing, cleaning, brewing) at the houses of the wealthy. The accounts here are much less familiar and (for their time) they may be unique.

Both Duck and Collier are concerned with the relation of labour to sociability. Duck professes to scorn the 'prattling females' who combine gossip with their work, and this is satirised as a feminine weakness. But Duck is not consistent here, for he has earlier lamented that the noisy work of threshing prevents the labourers from 'beguiling' the time by telling tales like shepherds. In the hay and harvest field, however, the emphasis is (with

Duck) upon male competitiveness in labour—

> As the best Man, each claims the foremost Place,
> And our first Work seems but a sportive Race . . .

At noon the male labourers retire, too exhausted (it seems) to do more than drink and 'faintly eat'. Whereas the women are always able to 'chat'. Collier, by contrast, will not apologise for the intermingling of work and sociability. She perhaps gives a little ground to the male stereotype of feminine gossip ('The only Privilege our Sex enjoy'), but then she goes over to a spirited defence:

> For none but *Turks*, that I could ever find,
> Have Mutes to serve them, or did e'er deny
> Their Slaves, at Work, to chat it merrily.

What emerges from Duck's poem is a greater sense of the imposition of work-discipline and a greater sensitivity to the employer's disapproval. The threshers submit to their master's curses 'just like School-boys'. The male labourers, possibly, were more aware of their vulnerability to dismissal if they offended the master; whereas the women, whose labour was more occasional or seasonal but whose labour was indispensable during the hay and cereal harvests, were, in a sense, in a stronger position. This might suggest that the male labourer, in selling his labour, must sell at the same time his right to express himself in other ways; he must curb his sociability, and this discipline made him resent the 'prattling Females' who had sold only their labour for a few weeks, and who maintained what was now seen as a 'female privilege'.

A related question is the degree of deference expressed in the two poems. Of course, neither poet questions the necessity of wage-labour. But, contrary to one stereotype, the woman's poem is less deferential than the man's. And yet this is because—and here we do return to an old stereotype—the woman views her situation less impersonally, more 'subjectively', than the man.

In Duck's poem the 'Master' appears—whether cheerful or cursing—as a scarcely-personal element in the labourers' situation, like the weather. He is defined by his role, and while there is an undercurrent of resentment (the Master's curses are unfair, the inversion of the harvest-home is a

'Cheat') this resentment is not personalised nor is it even generalised into a class complaint, except at the 'painful' lot of Labour. The gentry do not appear in Duck's poem at all, except in the deferential invocation to a patron (the Reverend Stanley) with which the poem starts. And a little resentment expressed against a farmer-employer would cause no offence to a genteel reader, since in paternalism's self-image it was the duty of the rich to protect the poor from the grasping middling ranks.

Collier's poem is sharper. She shows no resentment at the farmer; one suspects that she rather enjoys the sociable weeks of harvest, despite the heavy work. But with 'charing' at the great house we enter another world, and a world in which we are situated within the perceptions of an underpaid and overworked labouring woman who is confronting an overprivileged Mistress and who sees her not only in her role as an employer but also as another woman. She has already laboured 'with the utmost Skill and Care' at the difficult and luxurious laundry (cambricks, muslins 'which our Ladies wear', 'Fashions which our Forefathers never knew')—she has already laboured for some hours before her Mistress (a 'drowsy Mortal') gets up and appears with '*perhaps* a Mug of Ale', and with, certainly, a string of superfluous commands. When she is cleaning the pans and pewter, 'Trumpery' is brought in 'to make complete our Slavery'. The language implies questions as to the humanity of class divisions, and as to the rationality of luxuries which depend upon the degrading labour of others. What make for the feminine 'Perfections' of the Mistress obscure the feminine nature of the labourer. The great house is seen as self-centred and insensitive, summoning labour at any hour of the night to meet its occasions. The final quatrain of Collier's poem takes this personal confrontation between two women to the point of explicit generalisation:

> So the industrious Bees do hourly strive
> To bring their Loads of Honey to the Hive;
> Their sordid Owners always reap the Gains,
> And poorly recompense their Toil and Pains.

Mary Collier was not only writing searchingly about gender roles but she was writing irreverently about the oppressions and the sensibility of class as well. These closing couplets may have been suggested to her directly by her countrywoman's experience. Yet they could also be read as an allusion to Bernard Mandeville's 'The Fable of the Bees', whose provocations became the subject of debate and of scandal in the decade after 1723. Could she have read this, or listened in on the debate about the relation between private vices ('Millions endeavouring to supply / Each other's Lust and Vanity') and public benefits? Mandeville argued that luxury (fueled by avarice, pride, prodigality, &c) created employment and national wealth. Collier shows us the underside of luxury, in the laundry and the kitchens, and also the humbug about 'national' wealth. Mandeville's hive has no owner (or it is owned by the bees) whereas Collier's does, and they are 'sordid'. Whether Collier was alluding to this debate at the origin of capitalist political economy or not, the lack of deference in her poem may explain why the little patronage which she received fell far short of the translation of the Reverend Stephen Duck.

E.P.T.

POEMS

ON

SEVERAL OCCASIONS.

By the REVEREND

Mr. STEPHEN DUCK.

The THIRD EDITION.

LONDON:

Printed for SAMUEL BIRT, in *Ave-Mary Lane;*
T. LONGMAN, C. HITCH and L. HAWES, in
Pater-noster-row; JAMES HODGES, near *London-
Bridge;* and JOHN and JAMES RIVINGTON, in
S*t*. *Paul's Church-yard.*

M DCC LIII.

The THRESHER'S LABOUR

The grateful Tribute of these rural Lays,
Which to her Patron's hand the Muse conveys,
Deign to accept; 'tis just she Tribute bring
To him whose Bounty gives her Life to sing:
To him whose generous Favours tune her Voice,
And bid her 'midst her Poverty rejoice.
Inspir'd by these, she dares herself prepare,
To sing the Toils of each revolving Year:
Those endless Toils, which always grow anew,
And the poor Thresher's destin'd to pursue.
Ev'n these with pleasure can the Muse rehearse,
When You, and Gratitude, command the Verse.

Soon as the Harvest hath laid bare the Plains,
And Barns well fill'd reward the Farmer's pains;
What Corn each sheaf will yield, intent to hear,
And guess from thence the Profits of the year;
Or else impending Ruin to prevent,
By paying, timely, threat'ning Landlord's rent,
He calls his Threshers forth. Around we stand,
With deep attention, waiting his command.

1

To each our tasks he readily divides,
And pointing, to our different stations guides.
As he directs, to different Barns we go,
Here two for Wheat, and there for Barley two.
But first, to show what he expects to find,
These words, or words like these, disclose his Mind:
So dry the Corn was carried from the Field,
So easily 'twill thresh, so well 'twill yield.
Sure large day's Work I well may hope for now;
Come, strip, and try, let's see what you can do.

    Divested of our cloaths, with Flail in hand,
At a just distance, front to front we stand,
And first the Threshall's gently swung, to prove
Whether with just exactness it will move.
That once secure, more quick we whirl them round,
From the strong planks our Crab-tree Staves rebound,
And echoing Barns return the rattling sound.
Now in the air our knotty Weapons fly,
And now with equal force descend from high.
Down one, one up, so well they keep the Time,
The *Cyclops'* Hammers could not truer chime,
Nor with more heavy strokes could *Aetna* groan,
When *Vulcan* forg'd the arms for *Thetis'* Son.
In briny streams our sweat descends apace,
Drops from our locks, or trickles down our face.
No intermission in our Works we know;
The noisy Threshall must for ever go.
Their Master absent, others safely play;
The sleeping Threshall doth itself betray.
Nor yet the tedious Labour to beguile,
And make the passing Minutes sweetly smile,
Can we, like Shepherds, tell a merry tale?
The voice is lost, drown'd by the noisy Flail.

But we may think—alas! what pleasing thing
Here to the Mind can the dull Fancy bring?
The eye beholds no pleasant object here;
No cheerful sound diverts the list'ning ear.
The Shepherd well may tune his voice to sing,
Inspir'd by all the beauties of the Spring:
No Fountains murmur here, no Lambkins play,
No Linets warble, and no Fields look gay.
'Tis all a dull and melancholy Scene,
Fit only to provoke the Muses' Spleen.

When sooty Pease we thresh, you scarce can know
Our native colour, as from Work we go;
The sweat, and dust, and suffocating smoke
Make us so much like *Ethiopians* look,
We scare our Wives, when Evening brings us home,
And frighted Infants think the Bug-bear come.
Week after week we this dull Task pursue,
Unless when winnowing days produce a new,
A new indeed, but frequently a worse;
The Threshall yields but to the Master's Curse:
He counts the Bushels, counts how much a day,
Then swears we've idled half our Time away.
Why look ye, Rogues! D'ye think that this will do?
Your Neighbours thresh as much again as you.
Now in our hands we wish our noisy Tools,
To drown the hated Names of Rogues and Fools;
But wanting those, we just like School-boys look,
When th'angry Master views the blotted Book:
They cry their Ink was faulty, and their Pen;
We, the Corn threshes bad, 'twas cut too green.

But now the Winter hides his hoary head,
And Nature's face is with new Beauty spread;
The Spring appears, and kind refreshing Showers
New clothe the Field with Grass, and deck with Flowers.
Next her, the ripening Summer presses on,
And *Sol* begins his longest Stage to run.
Before the door our welcome Master stands,
And tells us the ripe Grass requires our hands.
The long much-wish'd Intelligence imparts
Life to our looks, and spirit to our hearts:
We wish the happy Season may be fair,
And joyful, long to breathe in opener Air.
This Change of Labour seems to give much Ease;
With thoughts of happiness our Joy's complete.
There's always Bitter mingled with the Sweet.
When Morn does thro' the Eastern Windows peep,
Strait from our Beds we start, and shake off Sleep;
This new Employ with eager haste to prove,
This new Employ becomes so much our Love.
Alas! that human Joys shou'd change so soon.
Even this may bear another Face at Noon!

The Birds salute us as to Work we go,
And a new Life seems in our Breasts to glow.
A-cross one's shoulder hangs a Scythe well steel'd,
The Weapon destin'd to unclothe the Field;
T'other supports the Whetstone, Scrip, and Beer,
That for our Scythes, and these ourselves to chear.
And now the Field design'd our Strength to try
Appears, and meets at last our longing eye;
The Grass and Ground each chearfully surveys,
Willing to see which way th'Advantage lays.
As the best man, each claims the foremost place,

And our first work seems but a sportive Race.
With rapid force our well-whet Blades we drive,
Strain every nerve, and blow for blow we give:
Tho' but this Eminence the foremost gains,
Only t'excel the rest in Toil and Pains.
But when the scorching Sun is mounted high,
And no kind Barns with friendly Shades are nigh,
Our weary Scythes entangle in the grass,
And streams of sweat run trickling down apace;
Our sportive Labour we too late lament,
And wish that Strength again we vainly spent.

    Thus in the Morn a Courser I have seen,
With headlong Fury scour the level Green,
Or mount the Hills, if Hills are in his way,
As if no Labour could his fire allay,
Till the meridian Sun with sultry Heat
And piercing Beams hath bath'd his sides in sweat;
The lengthen'd Chace scarce able to sustain,
He measures back the Hills and Dales with pain.

    With Heat and Labour tir'd, our Scythes we quit,
Search out a shady tree, and down we sit;
From Scrip and Bottle hope new Strength to gain,
But Scrip and Bottle too are try'd in vain.
Down our parch'd throats we scarce the bread can get,
And quite o'er-spent with Toil, but faintly eat;
Nor can the Bottle only answer all,
Alas! the Bottle and the Beer's too small.
Our time slides on, we move from off the Grass,
And each again betakes him to his place.
Not eager now, as late, our strength to prove,
But all contented regular to move.
Often we whet, as often view the Sun,
To see how near his tedious race is run.
At length he vails his radiant face from sight,
And bids the weary Traveller good-night.
Homewards we move, but so much spent with toil,
We walk but slow, and rest at every Stile.
Our good expecting Wives, who think we stay,
Got to the door, soon eye us in the way;
Then from the pot the dumpling's catch'd in haste,
And homely by its side the bacon's plac'd.
Supper and sleep by Morn new strength supply,
And out we set again our works to try,
But not so early quite, nor quite so fast,
As to our cost we did the Morning past.

Soon as the rising Sun hath drunk the dew
Another scene is open'd to our view:
Our Master comes, and at his Heels a Throng
Of prattling Females, arm'd with Rake and Prong,
Prepar'd, whil'st he is here, to make his Hay,
Or, if he turns his back, prepar'd to play.
But here, or gone, sure of this comfort still,
Here's Company, so they may chat their fill:
And were their Hands as active as their Tongues,
How nimbly then would move their Rakes and Prongs?
The Grass again is spread upon the Ground,
Till not a vacant place is to be found,
And while the piercing sunbeams on it shine,
The Haymakers have time allow'd to dine.
That soon dispatch'd, they still sit on the Ground,
And the brisk Chat renew'd, afresh goes round;
All talk at once, but seeming all to fear
That all they speak so well, the rest won't hear.
By quick degrees so high their notes they strain,
That Standers-by can naught distinguish plain.
So loud their Speech, and so confus'd their Noise,
Scarce puzzled Echo can return a Voice;
Yet spite of this, they bravely all go on,
Each scorns to be, or seem to be, outdone,
Till (unobserv'd before) a low'ring Sky,
Fraught with black Clouds, proclaims a Shower nigh.
The tattling Crowd can scarce their garments gain,
Before descends the thick impetuous Rain;
Their noisy Prattle all at once is done,
And to the Hedge they all for Shelter run.

Thus have I seen on a bright Summer's day,
On some green brake a Flock of Sparrows play.
From twig to twig, from bush to bush they fly,
And with continu'd chirping fill the Sky,
But on a sudden, if a Storm appears,
Their chirping noise no longer dins your ears;

They fly for shelter to the thickest bush,
Their silent sit, and all at once is hush.
But better Fate succeeds this rainy Day,
And little Labour serves to make the Hay;
Fast as 'tis cut, so kindly shines the Sun,
Turn'd once or twice, the pleasing Work is done.
Next day the Cocks appear in equal Rows,
Which the glad Master in safe Ricks bestows.

    But now the Field we must no longer range,
And yet, hard Fate! still Work for Work we change.
Back to the Barns again in haste we're sent,
Where lately so much time we pensive spent;
Not pensive now, we bless the friendly Shade,
And to avoid the parching Sun are glad.
But few days here we're destin'd to remain,
Before our Master calls us forth again:
For Harvest now, says he, yourselves prepare,
The ripen'd Harvest now demands your Care.
Early next Morn I shall disturb your rest,
Get all things ready, and be quickly drest.

Strict to his word, scarce the next dawn appears,
Before his hasty Summons fills our ears.
Obedient to his call, strait up we get,
And finding soon our Company complete,
With him, our Guide, we to the Wheat-field go,
He to appoint and we the Work to do.
Ye Reapers, cast your eyes around the Field,
And view the scene its different Beauties yield;
Then look again with a more tender eye,
To think how soon it must in ruin lie.
For once set in, where-e'er our blows we deal,
There's no resisting of the well-whet Steel,
But here or there, where-e'er our Course we bend,
Sure Desolation does our steps attend.
Thus when *Arabia*'s sons, in hopes of prey,
To some more fertile Country take their way,
How beauteous all things in the Morn appear,
There villages, and pleasing cots are here;
So many pleasing objects meet the sight,
The ravish'd eye could willing gaze 'till Night,
But long ere then, where-e'er their Troops have past,
Those pleasant Prospects lie a gloomy Waste.

   The Morning past, we sweat beneath the Sun,
And but uneasily our Work goes on.
Before us we perplexing Thistles find,
And Corn blown adverse with the ruffling Wind.
Behind our backs the Female Gleaners wait,
Who sometimes stoop, and sometimes hold a Chat.
Each Morn we early rise, go late to bed,
And lab'ring hard, a painful life we lead.

For Toils, scarce ever ceasing, press us now,
Rest never does, but on the Sabbath show,
And barely that, our Master will allow.
Nor when asleep are we secure from Pain;
We then perform our Labours o'er again;
Our mimic Fancy always restless seems,
And what we act awake, she acts in Dreams.
Hard Fate! Our Labours ev'n in Sleep don't cease;
Scarce *Hercules* e'er felt such Toils as these.
At length in rows stands up the well-dry'd Corn,
A grateful Scene, and ready for the Barn.
Our well-pleas'd Master views the sight with joy,
And we for carrying all our force employ.
Confusion soon o'er all the Field appears,
And stunning Clamours fill the Workmen's ears;
The Bells and clashing Whips alternate sound,
And rattling Waggons thunder o'er the Ground.
The Wheat got in, the Pease and other Grain,
Share the same Fate, and soon leave bare the plain.
In noisy Triumph the last load moves on.
And loud Huzzas proclaim the Harvest's done.

   Our Master joyful at the welcome sight,
Invites us all to feast with him at Night.
A Table plentifully spread we find,
And jugs of humming Beer to cheer the Mind,
Which he, too generous, pushes on so fast,
We think no toils to come, nor mind the past.
But the next Morning soon reveals the Cheat,
When the same toils we must again repeat,
To the same Barns again must back return,
To labour there for room for next year's Corn.

Thus as the Year's revolving course goes round,
No respite from our Labour can be found.
Like *Sysiphus*, our Work is never done;
Continually rolls back the restless Stone.
Now growing Labours still succeed the past,
And growing always new, must always last.

THE

Woman's Labour:

AN

EPISTLE

TO

Mr. STEPHEN DUCK;

In ANSWER to his late Poem, called
THE THRESHER'S LABOUR.

To which are added,

The Three WISE SENTENCES,

TAKEN FROM

The First Book of ESDRAS, Ch. III. and IV.

By *MARY COLLIER*,
Now a WASHER-WOMAN, at *Petersfield* in *Hampshire*.

LONDON,

Printed for the AUTHOR ; and fold by J. ROBERTS,
in *Warwick-lane* ; and at the Pamphlet-Shops near
the *Royal Exchange.* 1739.

Price Six-Pence.

The WOMAN'S LABOUR

Immortal Bard! thou fav'rite of the Nine!
Enrich'd by Peers, advanc'd by Caroline,
Deign to look down on one that's poor and low,
Remembering you yourself was lately so;
Accept these lines: alas! what can you have
From her, who ever was, and's still a Slave?
No Learning ever was bestow'd on me;
My life was always spent in Drudgery,
And not alone; alas! with grief I find
It is the Portion of poor Woman-kind.
Oft have I thought as on my bed I lay,
Eas'd from the tiresome Labours of the day,
Our first Extraction from a Mass refin'd
Could never be for Slavery design'd,
Till Time and Custom by degrees destroy'd
That happy state our Sex at first enjoy'd.
When Men had used their utmost care and toil,
Their Recompence was but a Female Smile;

When they by Arts or Arms were rendered great,
They laid their Trophies at a Woman's Feet.
They, in those days, unto our Sex did bring
Their Hearts, their All, a free-will Offering,
And as from us their Being they derive,
They back again should all due Homage give.

    Jove once descending from the clouds did drop
In show'rs of gold on lovely *Danae*'s lap;
The sweet-tongu'd Poets, in those generous days,
Unto our Shrine still offer'd up their Lays:
But now, alas! that Golden Age is past,
We are the objects of your Scorn at last.
    And you, great Duck, upon whose happy brow
The Muses seem to fix the Garland now,
In your late Poem boldly did declare
Alcides' Labours can't with yours compare;
And of your annual Task have much to say,
Of threshing, reaping, mowing Corn and Hay,
Boasting your daily Toil and nightly Dream,
But can't conclude your never-dying Theme,
And let our hapless Sex in Silence lie
Forgotten, and in dark Oblivion die;
But on our abject State you throw your Scorn,
And Women wrong, your Verses to adorn.
    You of Hay-making speak a word or two,
As if our Sex but little Work could do:
This makes the honest Farmer smiling say
He'll seek for Women still to make his Hay;
For if his back be turn'd, their Work they mind
As well as Men, as far as he can find.

    For my own part, I many a Summer's day
Have spent in throwing, turning, making Hay,
But ne'er could see, what you have lately found,
Our Wages paid for sitting on the Ground.
'Tis true, that when our Morning's Work is done,
And all our Grass expos'd unto the Sun,
While that his scorching Beams do on it shine,
As well as you, we have a time to dine:

I hope that since we freely toil and sweat
To earn our Bread, you'll give us time to eat.
That over, soon we must get up again,
And nimbly turn our Hay upon the plain,
Nay, rake and prow it in, the case is clear,
Or how should Cocks in equal Rows appear?
But if you'd have what you have wrote believ'd,
I find that you to hear us talk are griev'd.
In this, I hope, you do not speak your mind,
For none but *Turks*, that I could ever find,
Have Mutes to serve them, or did e'er deny
Their Slaves, at Work, to chat it merrily.
Since you have Liberty to speak your mind,
And are to talk, as well as we, inclin'd,
Why should you thus repine, because that we,
Like you, enjoy that pleasing Liberty?
What! would you lord it quite, and take away
The only Privilege our Sex enjoy?

When Evening does approach we homeward hie,
And our domestic Toils incessant ply:
Against your coming home prepare to get
Our Work all done, our House in order set.
Bacon and Dumpling in the pot we boil,
Our Beds we make, our Swine we feed the while,
Then wait at Door to see you coming home,
And set the Table out against you come.
Early next morning we on you attend;
Our Children dress and feed, their cloaths we mend,
And in the Field our daily Task renew,
Soon as the rising Sun has dry'd the Dew.

When Harvest comes, into the Field we go,
And help to reap the Wheat as well as you,
Or else we go the ears of Corn to glean,
No Labour scorning, be it e'er so mean,
But in the Work we freely bear a part,
And what we can, perform with all our Heart.

To get a living we so willing are,
Our tender Babes into the Field we bear,
And wrap them in our cloaths to keep them warm,
While round about we gather up the Corn,
And often unto them our course we bend,
To keep them safe, that nothing them offend.
Our Children that are able, bear a share
In gleaning Corn, such is our frugal care.
When Night comes on, unto our home we go,
Our Corn we carry, and our Infant too;
Weary, alas! but 'tis not worth our while
Once to complain, or *rest at ev'ry Stile.*
We must make haste, for when we Home are come,
Alas! we find our Work but just begun;
So many things for our Attendance call,
Had we ten hands, we could employ them all.
Our Children put to bed, with greatest care,
We all things for your coming Home prepare:
You sup, and go to bed without delay,
And rest yourselves till the ensuing Day,
While we, alas! but little Sleep can have,
Because our froward Children cry and rave.
Yet without fail, soon as Daylight doth spring,
We in the Field again our Work begin,
And there with all our Strength our Toil renew,
Till *Titan*'s golden rays have dry'd the Dew.
Then home we go unto our Children dear,
Dress, feed, and bring them to the Field with care.
Were this your case, you justly might complain
That Day nor Night you are secure from Pain;
Those mighty Troubles which perplex your Mind,
(*Thistles* before, and *Females* come behind)
Would vanish soon, and quickly disappear,
Were you, like us, encumber'd thus with Care.

What you would have of us we do not know:
We oft take up the Corn that you do mow,
We cut the Peas, and always ready are
In ev'ry Work to take our proper Share,
And from the time that Harvest doth begin,
Until the Corn be cut and carry'd in,
Our Toil and Labour's daily so extreme
That we have hardly ever *Time to dream.*

    The Harvest ended, respite none we find,
The hardest of our Toil is still behind:
Hard Labour we most chearfully pursue,
And out abroad, a-charring often go,
Of which I now will briefly tell in part
What fully to declare is past my Art,
So many Hardships daily we go through,
I boldly say, the like *you* never knew.

    When bright *Orion* glitters in the skies
In Winter nights, then early we must rise;
The Weather ne'er so bad, wind, rain or snow,
Our Work appointed, we must rise and go,
While you on easy beds may lie and sleep,
Till Light does thro' your Chamber-windows peep.
When to the House we come where we should go,
How to get in, alas! we do not know:
The Maid quite tir'd with Work the day before,
O'ercome with sleep; we standing at the door,
Oppress'd with cold, and often call in vain,
Ere to our Work we can Admittance gain.
But when from Wind and Weather we get in,
Briskly with Courage we our Work begin.
Heaps of find Linen we before us view,
Whereon to lay our Strength and Patience too:
Cambricks and Muslins, which our Ladies wear,
Laces and Edgings, costly, fine, and rare,
Which must be wash'd with utmost Skill and Care.
With Holland Shirts, Ruffles and Fringes too,
Fashions which our Forefathers never knew.

For several hours here we work and slave,
Before we can one glimpse of Daylight have.
We labour hard before the Morning's past,
Because we fear the time runs on too fast.
    At length bright *Sol* illuminates the skies,
And summons drowsy Mortals to arise.
Then comes our Mistress to us without fail,
And in her hand, *perhaps*, a mug of Ale
To cheer our Hearts, and also to inform
Herself, what Work is done that very Morn;
Lays her Commands upon us, that we mind
Her Linen well, nor *leave the Dirt behind.*
Not this alone, but also to take care
We don't her Cambricks or her Ruffles tear,
And these most strictly does of us require:
To save her Soap, and sparing be of Fire;
Tells us her Charge is great, nay, furthermore,
Her Cloaths are fewer than the time before.

Now we drive on, resolv'd our Strength to try,
And what we can, we do most willingly,
Until the Heat and Work, 'tis often known,
Not only Sweat but Blood runs trickling down
Our wrists and fingers; still our Work demands
The constant action of our lab'ring Hands.

    Now Night comes on, from whence you have Relief,
But that, alas! does but increase our Grief.
With heavy hearts we often view the Sun,
Fearing he'll set before our Work is done;
For either in the Morning, or at Night,
We piece the Summer's day with Candle-light.
Tho' we all Day with care our Work attend,
Such is our Fate, we know not when 'twill end.
When Evening's come you Homeward take your way;
We till our Work is done are forc'd to stay,
And after all our Toil and Labour past,
Sixpence or Eightpence pays us off at last.
For all our Pains, no Prospect can we see
Attend us, but Old Age and Poverty.

    The Washing is not all we have to do:
We oft change Work for Work as well as you.
Our Mistress of her Pewter doth complain,
And 'tis our part to make it clean again.
This Work, tho' very hard and tiresome too,
Is not the worst we hapless Females do.
When Night comes on, and we quite weary are,
We scarce can count what falls unto our Share:
Pots, kettles, sauce-pans, skillets we may see,
Skimmers and ladles and such Trumpery,
Brought in to make complete our Slavery.
Tho' early in the Morning 'tis begun,
'Tis often very late before we've done.

Alas! our Labours never know an end:
On brass and iron we our Strength must spend,
Our tender hands and fingers scratch and tear;
All this and more, with Patience we must bear.
Colour'd with Dirt and Filth we now appear;
Your threshing sooty Peas will not come near.
All the Perfections Woman once could boast
Are quite obscur'd, and altogether lost.

Once more our Mistress sends to let us know
She wants our Help, because the Beer runs low.
Then in much haste for Brewing we prepare,
The Vessels clean, and scald with greatest care.
Often at Midnight from our bed we rise;
At other times ev'n that will not suffice;
Our Work at Evening oft we do begin,
And ere we've done, the Night comes on again.
Water we pump, the Copper we must fill,
Or tend the Fire, for if we e'er stand still,
Like you when threshing, we a Watch must keep;
Our Wort boils over if we dare to sleep.

But to rehearse all Labour is in vain
Of which we very justly might complain:
For us, you see, but little rest is found,
Our Toil increases as the Year runs round.
While you to *Sysiphus* yourselves compare,
With *Danaus'* daughters we may claim a share;
For while *he* labours hard against the Hill,
Bottomless Tubs of Water *they* must fill.

So the industrious Bees do hourly strive
To bring their Loads of Honey to the Hive;
Their sordid Owners always reap the Gains,
And poorly recompense their Toil and Pains.

ADVERTISEMENT.

IT is thought proper to aſſure the Reader, that the following Verſes are the real Productions of the Perſon to whom the Title-Page aſcribes them.

THO' She pretends not to the Genius of Mr. DUCK, nor hopes to be taken Notice of by the Great, yet her Friends are of Opinion that the Novelty of a *Waſher-Woman*'s turning Poeteſs, will procure her ſome Readers.

IF all that follow the ſame Employment would amuſe themſelves, and one another, during the tedious Hours of their Labour, in this, or ſome other Way as innocent, inſtead of toſſing Scandal to and fro, many Reputations would remain unwounded, and the Peace of Families be leſs diſturb'd.

A 2

I

ADVERTISEMENT.

I THINK it no Reproach to the Author, whofe Life is toilfome, and her Wages inconfiderable, to confefs honeftly, that the View of her putting a fmall Sum of Money in her Pocket, as well as the Reader's Entertainment, had its Share of Influence upon this Publication. And fhe humbly hopes fhe fhall not be abfolutely difappointed; fince, tho' fhe is ready to own that her Performance could by no Means ftand a critical Examination, yet fhe flatters herfelf that, with all its Faults and Imperfections, the candid Reader will judge it to be Something confiderably beyond the common Capacity of thofe of her own Rank and Occupation.

M. B.

EDITORIAL NOTE

We have wanted to present these poems to the non-specialist reader in the most easily available form, while maintaining authenticity. This has led us to adopt hybrid editorial practices which may not please the purist; we have not always followed the original capitalisation (where it made for self-consciously cumbersome reading), and we have very occasionally modernised punctuation and spelling.

Facsimile reprints of both poems are obtainable: Stephen Duck's *Poems on Several Occasions* (1736), reproduced by the Scolar Press (Menston, Yorkshire, 1973) with an introduction by John Lucas, and both *The Thresher's Labour* and *The Woman's Labour*, reproduced by the Augustan Reprint Society, no. 230 (William Andrews Clark Memorial Library, Los Angeles, 1985) with an introduction by Moira Ferguson.

In terms of authenticity our edition of Duck may be an improvement on these. We have preferred to depend upon a 1730 edition of *The Thresher's Labour*, whereas both facsimiles take their version from the 1736 *Poems on Several Occasions*. This is formally correct, because this is the first edition authorised by the poet himself. Under the title *Poems on Several Subjects* Duck's early poems were pirated, and went through at least seven editions in 1730, and further editions in 1731 and 1733. In 1734 Duck wrote that *The Thresher's Labour* had never been published with his approbation. In his preface to the 1736 *Poems* he appears to apologise for the delay in preparing his own edition, because of the time he had spent, since 1730, 'in endeavouring to learn a Language, of which I was then intirely ignorant'. This language was Latin. *The Thresher's Labour* appears to have been 'corrected' in the light of Duck's intervening classical education.

The 1730 edition which we have used may have been pirated, but there is no reason for doubting its authenticity.

27

We take it to be a true copy of the poem in its original state. Only thirteen lines into the poem we can see what a classical 'correction' entails.

> Soon as the Harvest hath laid bare the Plains,
> And Barns well fill'd reward the Farmer's Pains . . .

('our' edition, 1730) becomes, in 1736:

> Soon as the golden Harvest quits the Plain,
> And *Ceres'* Gifts reward the Farmer's Pain . . .

Visually, the original conveys the clearance of the harvest fields, laying them 'bare', and preparing the imagination for autumn and the Lammas turning-in of stock. All is personification in the 1736 version—not only Ceres, but even the 'Harvest' which 'quits the Plain' without human intervention. The 'Farmer's Pain' is abstract in comparison with his 'Pains', which include in our 1730 edition his fear of 'impending Ruin' and the threatening 'Landlord's Rent', a couplet which is simply dropped (on the advice of one of Duck's invigilatory patrons?) in 1736.

The changes between 1730 and 1736 are not extensive, but several more may be noted. In 1730

> When Morn does thro' the Eastern Windows peep,
> Strait from our Beds we start, and shake off Sleep . . .

But in 1736

> When first the Lark sings Prologue to the Day,
> We rise, admonish'd by his early Lay . . .

Neither couplet is remarkable, but it is not difficult to decide which is closer to the labourer's experience. It is sad to observe how Duck is modifying his poem in order to cast himself as a figure in pastoral. In 1730 he sets out to work with 'Across one's Shoulder . . . a Scythe well steel'd', but in 1736 it has become 'a crooked Blade'; the reason for this may be that the 'Weapon destin'd to unclothe the Field' (1730) must in 1736 unclothe 'the Mead', and 'Blade' is required as a rhyme. The blades are 'well-whet' in 1730, but only 'sharpen'd' in 1736, perhaps because 'whet' is an unpoetic, rustic term? The 'meridian Sun' of 1730 gives way to 'Phoebus' in 1736, and for some reason his 'radiant' face has in the interval become 'purple'.

There is also some re-working in the last two pages of the poem. The chattering female gleaners of 1730 are dropped in 1736, and in place of them we have a reference to the farmer overseeing the reapers in the harvest field:

> Behind our Master waits; and if he spies
> One charitable Ear, he grudging cries,
> 'Ye scatter half your Wages o'er the Land'.
> Then scrapes the Stubble with his greedy Hand.

In this case the revision takes us closer to actual agrarian practice. Gleaners would not have been following behind the backs of the reapers, since it was normally the custom not to permit gleaning until the harvest had been carried. In 1730 Duck had been eliding two labour processes: first, the women's labour of gathering the sheaves into stooks, ready for carrying, and secondly the gleaning. It was often alleged that the reapers deliberately scattered some ears on the ground for the subsequent gleaning, and they probably did. There can be no objection to the 1736 revision in this instance, although Mary Collier's description of women's work in the cereal harvest and in gleaning makes it clear that she was answering the 1730 and not the 1736 edition.

The final harvest-home passage is much the same in both versions, except for an irritating classical emendation at its start.

> At length in Rows stands up the well-dry'd Corn,
> A grateful Scene, and ready for the Barn . . . (1730)

becomes in 1736:

> But soon we rise the bearded Crop again,
> Soon PHOEBUS' Rays well dry the golden Grain.

The sad case of Stephen Duck is that after 1730 he was writing more and more in the latter style.

Biographical sources for Duck include J[oseph] S[pence], *A Full and Authentick Account of Stephen Duck, the Wiltshire Poet*, (London, 1731), which was reprinted as a foreword to the 1736 *Poems*. The pirated seventh and later editions (1730 c) of *Poems* included a four-page 'Life' by a person who (Duck wrote in 1736) 'seems to have had as little Regard for Truth, as he had for Honesty, when he stole my Poems'. Robert Southey in *The Lives and Works of the Uneducated Poets* drew upon both accounts. A careful study by Rose Mary Davis, *Stephen Duck, the Thresher Poet*, was published in the University of Maine Studies, second series, no. 8, January 1927.

We have used here the first edition of Mary Collier's *The Woman's Labour* (1739). Very little has, as yet, been discovered about her. It seems that her very existence was doubted, since 'a new edition' (Petersfield, n.d., but perhaps 1765) includes an affidavit, dated 21 Stepember 1739, from nine prominent inhabitants of Petersfield, Hants, to the effect that she was 'the real author' of the poems. Both this and a 1762 edition include 'Some Remarks of the Author's Life drawn by Herself'.

The editions of Duck and of Collier which we have used are in the British Library. Our frontispiece, showing the poet with a threshall in one hand and a volume of Milton in the other, with his writing table in the farmyard at the barn door, was the frontispiece of the seventh edition (1730) of Duck's *Poems*. The 1753 edition includes an engraving of a portrait of Duck by Sir James Thornhill. No picture of Mary Collier survives.

M.S. and E.P.T.